THE NACHO COOKBOOK

50 DELICIOUS NACHO RECIPES

By
BookSumo Press

Published by
BookSumo Press, a DBA of Saxonberg Associates
http://www.booksumo.com/

ABOUT THE AUTHOR.

BookSumo Press is a publisher of unique, easy, and healthy cookbooks.

Our cookbooks span all topics and all subjects. If you want a deep dive into the possibilities of cooking with any type of ingredient. Then BookSumo Press is your go to place for robust yet simple and delicious cookbooks and recipes. Whether you are looking for great tasting pressure cooker recipes or authentic ethic and cultural food. BookSumo Press has a delicious and easy cookbook for you.

With simple ingredients, and even simpler step-by-step instructions BookSumo cookbooks get everyone in the kitchen chefing delicious meals.

BookSumo is an independent publisher of books operating in the beautiful Garden State (NJ) and our team of chefs and kitchen experts are here to teach, eat, and be merry!

INTRODUCTION

Welcome to *The Effortless Chef Series*! Thank you for taking the time to purchase this cookbook.

Come take a journey into the delights of easy cooking. The point of this cookbook and all BookSumo Press cookbooks is to exemplify the effortless nature of cooking simply.

In this book we focus on Nacho. You will find that even though the recipes are simple, the taste of the dishes are quite amazing.

So will you take an adventure in simple cooking? If the answer is yes please consult the table of contents to find the dishes you are most interested in.

Once you are ready, jump right in and start cooking.

— BookSumo Press

TABLE OF CONTENTS

ANY ISSUES? CONTACT US

If you find that something important to you is missing from this book please contact us at info@booksumo.com.

We will take your concerns into consideration when the 2nd edition of this book is published. And we will keep you updated!

— BookSumo Press

LEGAL NOTES

COMMON ABBREVIATIONS

cup(s)	C.
tablespoon	tbsp
teaspoon	tsp
ounce	oz.
pound	lb

*All units used are standard American measurements

Chapter 1: Easy Nacho Recipes

Flavorful Nachos

Ingredients

- 1/2 lb. bacon, cooked and crumbled (divided)
- 1/2-3/4 C. red onion, chopped (divided)
- 1 medium tomato, seeded and chopped
- 1 (2 1/4 oz.) can sliced black olives
- 6 -7 jalapeno peppers, seeded and chopped (divided)
- 2 1/2 C. Mexican blend cheese (Shredded and divided)
- 9 oz. tortilla chips (divided)

Directions

- Set your oven to 425 degrees F before doing anything else and line a baking sheet with foil.
- Place half of the tortilla chips in the bottom of the prepared baking sheet evenly.
- Top everything with 1/2 of the bacon, followed by 1/2 of the onion and jalapeño peppers and about 1 C. of the cheese blend.

- Now, place the remaining tortilla chips, followed by the remaining bacon, onion, jalapeño peppers, olives, tomatoes and remaining cheese blend.
- Cook everything in the oven for about 5-10 minutes.

Amount per serving: 4

Timing Information:

| Preparation | 15 mins |
| Total Time | 25 mins |

Nutritional Information:

Calories	891.4
Fat	65.8g
Cholesterol	125.1mg
Sodium	1771.8mg
Carbohydrates	47.9g
Protein	29.6g

* Percent Daily Values are based on a 2,000 calorie diet.

MONTEREY CRAB AND SHRIMP NACHOS

Ingredients

- 1/2 lb. imitation crabmeat, shredded
- 1/2 lb. shrimp, cooked and chopped
- 1/2 C. low-fat sour cream
- 1 (4 1/2 oz.) can green chilies, diced
- 1 tsp chili powder
- 1/2 tsp ground cumin
- 1/4 tsp salt
- 1 C. salsa
- 1 C. shredded Monterey jack pepper cheese
- 1/2 C. black olives
- 2 scallions, sliced
- 1 (8 1/2 oz.) bags tortilla chips

Directions

- Set your oven to 350 degrees F before doing anything else.
- Place half of the tortilla chips in the bottom of a 13x9-inch baking dish evenly.
- Top the dish with the seafood mixture, followed by the salsa, cheese, olives and scallions.
- Cook everything in the oven for about 16 minutes.

Amount per serving: 6

Timing Information:

| Preparation | 10 mins |
| Total Time | 26 mins |

Nutritional Information:

Calories	377.0
Fat	18.7g
Cholesterol	79.8mg
Sodium	1244.6mg
Carbohydrates	37.2g
Protein	17.4g

* Percent Daily Values are based on a 2,000 calorie diet.

Restaurant-Quality Nachos

Ingredients

- 1 lb. lean ground beef
- 1 medium onion, finely chopped
- 1 -2 tbsp fresh minced garlic
- 1 jalapeno pepper, seeded and finely chopped
- 1 small green bell pepper, seeded and chopped
- 2 -3 tbsp chili powder
- 1 1/2 C. refried beans
- 1 (16 oz.) jars salsa
- 1 1/2 C. grated cheddar cheese, divided

- seasoning salt
- black pepper
- tortilla chips (as desired)

Toppings:

- 1 C. sour cream
- 3 -4 green onions, chopped
- 2 large firm plum tomatoes, finely chopped
- sliced black olives

Directions

- Heat a large skillet and cook the beef, onion, bell pepper, jalapeño peppers, garlic and chili powder till the beef is browned lightly.
- Discard all the fat from the skillet and cook everything till the beef becomes browned completely.

- Stir in the salsa and refried beans and continue cooking, stirring continuously, till everything is heated completely.
- Stir in about 3/4 cup of the cheese and cook, stirring continuously till melted completely.
- In a large serving platter, place the tortilla chips and top them with the beef mixture and the remaining cheese.
- Serve hot with a garnishing of all the topping ingredients.

Amount per serving: 6

Timing Information:

Preparation	20 mins
Total Time	20 mins

Nutritional Information:

Calories	421.6
Fat	25.7g
Cholesterol	98.7mg
Sodium	1024.1mg
Carbohydrates	20.8g
Protein	28.4g

* Percent Daily Values are based on a 2,000 calorie diet.

DESSERT NACHOS

Ingredients

- 3 C. sliced fresh strawberries
- 1/4 C. sugar
- 1/4 cup almond liqueur
- 3/4 C. sour cream
- 2 tbsp sugar
- 1/4 tsp cinnamon
- 6 6-inch flour tortillas

- 2 tbsp melted butter
- 2 tsp sugar
- 1/4 tsp cinnamon
- 2 tbsp sliced almonds, toasted
- 1 tbsp shaved semisweet chocolate

Directions

- In a bowl, mix together the strawberries, almond liqueur and 1/4 C. of the sugar and refrigerate, covered for about 1 hour.
- Set your oven to 400 degrees F.
- In a bowl, mix together the sour cream, 2 tbsp of the sugar and 1/4 tsp of the cinnamon and refrigerate before serving.
- With a pastry brush, coat 1 side of the tortillas with the melted butter and then cut each one into 6 wedges.
- Place the tortilla wedges in 2 ungreased baking sheets evenly and sprinkle them with 2 tsp of the sugar and 1/4 tsp of the cinnamon.

- Cook everything in the oven for about 6-8 minutes.
- Remove everything from the oven and keep it aside to cool.
- Drain the strawberries completely.
- In serving plates, divide the tortilla wedges and top them with the strawberries and sour cream mixture.
- Serve everything with a topping of toasted almonds and shaved chocolate.

Amount per serving: 6

Timing Information:

Preparation	1 hr 30 mins
Total Time	1 hr 38 mins

Nutritional Information:

Calories	284.3
Fat	14.0g
Cholesterol	22.8mg
Sodium	234.4mg
Carbohydrates	37.0g
Protein	4.5g

* Percent Daily Values are based on a 2,000 calorie diet.

REFRESHING NACHOS

Ingredients

- 1 C. salsa
- 1 cucumber, peeled and sliced
- 1/2 C. fat-free cheddar cheese, shredded
- 1/2 C. fat free sour cream

Directions

- In a strainer, place the salsa to drain slightly.
- In a 13x9-inch baking dish, arrange the cucumber slices in a single layer.
- Place about 1 tsp of the salsa over each cucumber slice and sprinkle each with the cheese.
- Place about 1 tsp of the sour cream over each slice and serve.

Amount per serving: 1

Timing Information:

Preparation	10 mins
Total Time	10 mins

Nutritional Information:

Calories	11.0
Fat	0.1g
Cholesterol	0.5mg
Sodium	78.6mg
Carbohydrates	2.2g
Protein	0.5g

* Percent Daily Values are based on a 2,000 calorie diet.

Classic Nachos

Ingredients

- 1 lb. ground turkey
- 1 (1 1/4 oz.) envelopes taco seasoning
- 3/4 C. water
- tortilla chips

- 1/2 C. sour cream
- 1/2 C. salsa
- 1/2 C. shredded Monterey jack cheese
- 1/2 C. shredded cheddar cheese

Directions

- Set the broiler of your oven and grease a baking sheet.
- Heat a large skillet on medium heat and cook the turkey until it is browned completely.
- Stir in the water and taco seasoning and simmer for about 15 minutes.
- Arrange the tortilla chips in the prepared baking dish and top them with turkey mixture, followed by the sour cream and salsa.
- Sprinkle everything with both cheeses and cook the nachos under the broiler for about 4-5 minutes.

Amount per serving: 6

Timing Information:

Preparation	15 mins
Total Time	20 mins

Nutritional Information:

Calories	232.6
Fat	16.2g
Cholesterol	86.4mg
Sodium	320.3mg
Carbohydrates	2.3g
Protein	18.8g

* Percent Daily Values are based on a 2,000 calorie diet.

SUPER-EASY NACHOS

Ingredients

- 4 tbsp butter
- 1 large onion
- 4 tbsp flour
- 2 C. milk
- 1 lb. cheddar cheese

Directions

- In a large skillet, melt the butter and sauté the onion till caramelized.
- Stir in the flour on medium heat and cook everything for about 2 minutes.
- Add the cheese and milk and cook, stirring continuously for about 15 minutes.

Amount per serving: 6

Timing Information:

Preparation	5 mins
Total Time	20 mins

Nutritional Information:

Calories	454.0
Fat	35.8g
Cholesterol	111.2mg
Sodium	578.8mg
Carbohydrates	11.0g
Protein	22.4g

* Percent Daily Values are based on a 2,000 calorie diet.

CREAM CHEESE NACHOS

Ingredients

- 1 (8 oz.) packages cream cheese, softened
- 1 (8 oz.) containers sour cream
- 1 (1 1/4 oz.) packages taco seasoning
- Shredded lettuce
- Chopped tomatoes
- Shredded cheese
- nacho chips

Directions

- In a blender, add sour cream, cream cheese and taco seasoning and pulse till smooth.
- Transfer the mixture in a pie dish and add tomatoes, lettuce and cheese.
- Refrigerate to chill before serving.
- Serve alongside the nacho chips.

Amount per serving: 4

Timing Information:

| Preparation | 10 mins |
| Total Time | 10 mins |

Nutritional Information:

Calories	326.3
Fat	31.2g
Cholesterol	93.5mg
Sodium	944.9mg
Carbohydrates	9.0g
Protein	4.6g

* Percent Daily Values are based on a 2,000 calorie diet.

Unique Nacho Joes

Ingredients

- 1 lb. ground beef
- 1 red onion, diced
- 1 green pepper, diced
- salt, to taste
- pepper, to taste
- 2 tbsp oil
- 2 tbsp garlic, minced
- 2 tsp Worcestershire sauce
- 1 (1 1/4 oz.) envelope taco seasoning
- 1 (16 oz.) jar salsa con queso, medium
- hamburger bun
- tortilla chips, for serving
- sour cream, if desired
- jalapeno pepper, if desired
- salsa, if desired
- shredded cheddar cheese, if desired

Directions

- In a large skillet, heat the oil and sauté the pepper and onion till tender.
- Add the beef, salt and black pepper and cook until it is browned completely.
- Stir in the garlic, taco seasoning and Worcestershire sauce and bring to a gentle simmer.
- Reduce the heat to low and stir in the salsa.

- Simmer for about 15 minutes
- Place the beef mixture over the buns alongside the jalapenos, sour cream and cheese or salsa.

Amount per serving: 4

Timing Information:

Preparation	10 mins
Total Time	30 mins

Nutritional Information:

Calories	329.5
Fat	23.9g
Cholesterol	77.1mg
Sodium	105.0mg
Carbohydrates	6.0g
Protein	21.8g

* Percent Daily Values are based on a 2,000 calorie diet.

Super-Bowl Nachos

Ingredients

- 2 large russet potatoes, scrubbed and chopped into thick wedges
- 2 -3 tsp vegetable oil
- 1/4 tsp garlic powder
- 1 tsp taco seasoning
- 1/4 C. black beans, rinsed and drained
- 2 tsp lime juice
- 1/4 tsp cumin
- 1/4 tsp chili powder
- cayenne pepper, to taste
- 1/2 medium tomatoes, diced
- 1 green onion, chopped
- 1 tbsp green chili, diced
- 2 tbsp shredded 4-cheese Mexican blend cheese

Directions

- Set your oven to 425 degrees F before doing anything else.
- In a baking dish, add the potatoes, taco seasoning, garlic powder and oil and toss to coat well.
- Now, place the potato wedges in a single layer and cook everything in the oven for about 25-30 minutes, stirring occasionally.
- Meanwhile in a pan, mix together the black beans, lime juice and spices on medium-low heat.
- Cook, stirring occasionally till majority of the liquid is absorbed.

- Remove everything from the heat and stir in the tomato, green chili and green onion.
- Remove the potatoes from the oven and immediately, sprinkle them with the cheese.
- Cook everything in the oven for about 1-2 minutes more.
- Top the potato wedges with the bean mixture and serve.

Amount per serving: 2

Timing Information:

Preparation	20 mins
Total Time	55 mins

Nutritional Information:

Calories	397.5
Fat	7.5g
Cholesterol	8.4mg
Sodium	158.8mg
Carbohydrates	73.3g
Protein	11.7g

* Percent Daily Values are based on a 2,000 calorie diet.

Southwest Nachos

Ingredients

- 1 C. diced tomatoes
- 1/4 C. diced green pepper
- 2 tbsp chopped ripe olives
- 2 tbsp chopped green chilies
- 2 tsp white vinegar
- 1/4 tsp garlic powder
- 1/8 tsp fresh ground pepper

- corn tortilla chips
- 1/4 C. shredded low-fat sharp cheddar cheese
- Corn Tortilla Chips
- 9 6-inch corn tortillas
- cold water

Directions

- Set your oven to 350 degrees F before doing anything else.
- Dip the tortillas in the cold water and then drain them on paper towels.
- Arrange the tortillas onto an ungreased baking sheet and cook everything in the oven for about 10 minutes.
- Remove everything from the oven and keep it aside to cool.
- With a biscuit cutter, cut the tortillas into 2 1/2-inch circles.
- Now, set the oven to broiler and arrange the oven rack about 6-inches from the heating element.

- In a large bowl, mix together the olives, green pepper, tomatoes, green chilies, garlic powder, black pepper and vinegar.
- Place about 2 tsp of the vegetables mixture on each tortilla chips and cook everything under the broiler till the cheese is melted.

Amount per serving: 1

Timing Information:

Preparation	10 mins
Total Time	20 mins

Nutritional Information:

Calories	18.9
Fat	0.3g
Cholesterol	0.2mg
Sodium	14.8mg
Carbohydrates	3.4g
Protein	0.7g

* Percent Daily Values are based on a 2,000 calorie diet.

SPEEDY NACHOS

Ingredients

- 1/2 lb. sliced bacon
- 36 tortilla chips
- 1 medium sweet onion (chopped)
- 6 pickled jalapeno peppers (stemmed, seeded & minced)
- 2 C. grated Monterey jack cheese
- 8 oz. sour cream
- mild salsa

Directions

- Set your oven to 475 degrees F before doing anything else.
- Heat a large skillet and cook the bacon until it is browned completely.
- Transfer the bacon onto a paper towel lined plate to drain and then chop it.
- In a large rimmed baking sheet, place the tortilla chips, followed by the bacon, onions, jalapeño peppers and cheese.
- Cook everything in the oven for about 5 minutes.
- Serve alongside the sour cream and salsa.

Amount per serving: 4

Timing Information:

| Preparation | 15 mins |
| Total Time | 20 mins |

Nutritional Information:

Calories	1750.0
Fat	109.4g
Cholesterol	119.9mg
Sodium	2360.6mg
Carbohydrates	160.0g
Protein	40.4g

* Percent Daily Values are based on a 2,000 calorie diet.

LATE-NIGHT NACHOS

Ingredients

- 2 C. prepared chili
- 7 oz. tortilla chips
- 2 C. shredded cheddar cheese
- salsa, to taste
- prepared guacamole, to taste
- sour cream

Directions

- Set your oven to 400 degrees F before doing anything else.
- In a microwave safe bowl, add the chili and microwave till heated completely.
- In the bottom of a 10-inch deep pie dish, place half of the tortilla chips, followed by half of the chili and half of the cheddar cheese
- Repeat the layering with the remaining ingredients.
- Cook everything in the oven for about 5 minutes.
- Serve immediately.

Amount per serving: 5

Timing Information:

| Preparation | 15 mins |
| Total Time | 22 mins |

Nutritional Information:

Calories	474.8
Fat	29.1g
Cholesterol	64.8mg
Sodium	968.4mg
Carbohydrates	36.6g
Protein	19.9g

* Percent Daily Values are based on a 2,000 calorie diet.

Thursday Night Nachos

Ingredients

- 2 lb. ground beef
- 1 (1 1/4 oz.) packages taco seasoning mix
- 1 1/2 C. water
- 1 (10 oz.) tortilla chips
- 2 C. grated cheddar cheese
- 2 small red onions, chopped
- 2 small ripe tomatoes, chopped
- 2 small avocados, chopped
- 2 C. shredded lettuce
- 1 C. sour cream
- 1/2 C. chopped black olives
- 1/4 C. jalapeno

Directions

- Heat a large skillet and cook the beef until it is browned completely.
- Drain the excess fat from the skillet.
- Stir in the water and taco mix and bring to a boil.
- Cook, stirring till liquid is absorbed.
- Transfer the beef into a large bowl.
- In another large bowl, place the tortilla chips.
- In small serving bowls, divide the remaining ingredients.
- Serve according to your own choice.

Amount per serving: 8

Timing Information:

Preparation	30 mins
Total Time	45 mins

Nutritional Information:

Calories	689.1
Fat	48.3g
Cholesterol	119.4mg
Sodium	497.3mg
Carbohydrates	32.3g
Protein	33.3g

* Percent Daily Values are based on a 2,000 calorie diet.

CRUNCHY MEXICAN SALAD

Ingredients

- 1 lb. lean ground beef
- 1/4 C. chopped onion
- 1 (1 1/4 oz.) packages taco seasoning
- 1 (8 oz.) cans tomato sauce
- 6 C. nacho cheese flavored tortilla chips, slightly crushed
- 4 -6 C. romaine lettuce, torn
- 1 -1 1/2 C. chopped tomato
- 1 large bell pepper, chopped
- 1/2 medium cucumber, thinly sliced
- 2 C. mild cheddar cheese, shredded
- sliced black olives, well drained
- salsa, to taste
- sour cream, to taste

Directions

- Heat a large skillet and cook the beef and onion until it is browned completely. Drain the excess fat from the skillet.
- Add the taco seasoning and cook, stirring for about 1 minute.
- Stir in the tomato sauce and bring to a boil.
- Reduce the heat and simmer everything, covered, for about 10 minutes, stirring occasionally.
- Divide the tortilla chips into serving plates and top them with the beef mixture, followed by the vegetables, lettuce and cheese.

- Serve everything with salsa and sour cream.

Amount per serving: 6

Timing Information:

Preparation	15 mins
Total Time	30 mins

Nutritional Information:

Calories	20.3g
Fat	88.6mg
Cholesterol	965.5mg
Sodium	10.8g
Carbohydrates	26.1g
Protein	20.3g

* Percent Daily Values are based on a 2,000 calorie diet.

GAME TIME NACHOS

Ingredients

- 3/4 lb. peeled deveined, cooked shrimp
- 1 1/2 C. shredded cheddar cheese
- 1 (4 oz.) cans chopped green chilies, drained
- 1/3 C. chopped green onion
- 1/4 C. sliced ripe olives, drained
- 1/2 C. mayonnaise
- 1/4 tsp ground cumin
- 48 tortilla chips, scoops

Directions

- Set your oven to 350 degrees F before doing anything else.
- In a large bowl, mix together the shrimp, olives, green chilies, green onion and cheese.
- In a small bowl, mix together the mayonnaise and cumin.
- Add the mayonnaise mixture in the bowl with shrimp mixture and mix well.
- Place about 1 tbsp of the shrimp mixture into each tortilla scoop.
- Arrange the scoops onto baking sheets and cook everything in the oven for about 5-10 minutes.
- Serve warm.

Amount per serving: 48

Timing Information:

Preparation	15 mins
Total Time	25 mins

Nutritional Information:

Calories	34.2
Fat	2.1g
Cholesterol	19.2mg
Sodium	111.8mg
Carbohydrates	1.0g
Protein	2.5g

* Percent Daily Values are based on a 2,000 calorie diet.

CRUNCHY NACHO CHICKEN

Ingredients

- 4 chicken breasts, pounded
- 1 C. mayonnaise
- 1 tsp italian seasoning
- 2 C. nacho cheese flavor Doritos, crushed
- 1/4 C. butter, melted

Directions

- Set your oven to 350 degrees F before doing anything else.
- Pound the chicken breasts till flatten slightly.
- In a shallow, dish mix together the mayonnaise and Italian Seasoning.
- In another shallow dish, place the crushed Doritos.
- Coat the chicken with the mayonnaise mixture and then roll into crushed Doritos.
- Arrange the chicken pieces in the casserole dish and drizzle with the melted butter.
- Cook everything in the oven for about 30 minutes.

Amount per serving: 4

Timing Information:

Preparation	10 mins
Total Time	40 mins

Nutritional Information:

Calories	580.2
Fat	44.5g
Cholesterol	138.5mg
Sodium	610.3mg
Carbohydrates	14.0g
Protein	30.8g

* Percent Daily Values are based on a 2,000 calorie diet.

CRISPY NACHOS

Ingredients

- 20 pieces triscuits
- 1/4 C. salsa
- 6 oz. low-fat cheddar cheese, thinly sliced

Directions

- Set the oven to broiler and arrange the oven rack about 4-inches from the heating element.
- In a baking pan, arrange the triscuits.
- Place about 1/4 tsp of the salsa over each triscuit, followed by a thin slice of cheddar cheese.
- Cook everything under the broiler for about 2-4 minutes.

Amount per serving: 2

Timing Information:

Preparation	5 mins
Total Time	7 mins

Nutritional Information:

Calories	156.1
Fat	6.0g
Cholesterol	17.8mg
Sodium	715.6mg
Carbohydrates	3.6g
Protein	21.2g

* Percent Daily Values are based on a 2,000 calorie diet.

Kid's Favorite Nachos

Ingredients

- 2 tbsp unsalted butter, melted
- 3 (7 -8 inch) flour tortillas
- 1/4 C. cinnamon sugar
- 1/4 C. heavy cream
- 1/2 C. semi-sweet chocolate chips
- 1 kiwi, peeled and diced
- 1 mango, peeled and diced
- 1/2 C. strawberry, diced
- 1/4 C. sweetened coconut, toasted
- sweetened whipped cream, to garnish

Directions

- Set your oven to 400 degrees F before doing anything else.
- Coat both sides of the tortillas with the butter and cinnamon sugar, then cut each tortilla into eighths.
- Arrange the tortillas in a baking sheet and cook everything in the oven for about 10 minutes.

- In a microwave safe bowl, add the cream and microwave till heated.
- Immediately, add the chocolate chips and keep everything aside for about 2 minutes.
- Microwave the mix for about 20 seconds.
- In a bowl, mix together the strawberries, mango and kiwi.
- In a large serving platter, place the tortilla chips, followed by the fruit mixture.
- Drizzle the dish with the chocolate sauce and serve with a topping of toasted coconut and whipped cream.

Amount per serving: 3

Timing Information:

Preparation	30 mins
Total Time	35 mins

Nutritional Information:

Calories	625.3
Fat	29.9g
Cholesterol	47.5mg
Sodium	346.4mg
Carbohydrates	89.8g
Protein	7.5g

* Percent Daily Values are based on a 2,000 calorie diet.

ALPINE SWISS NACHOS

Ingredients

- 2 1/2 C. refried beans
- 5 -6 oz. tortilla chips
- 1 C. swiss cheese, grated
- 1 C. provolone cheese, grated
- 1 jalapeno, stemmed, seeded and diced
- 1/2 C. sour cream
- 1 tbsp pimiento, drained and chopped (jarred)

Directions

- Set your oven to 300 degrees F before doing anything else.
- In a pan, add the refried beans on medium heat and cook till heated completely.
- In a large oval baking dish, place the tortilla chips, followed by the beans and cheese.
- Cook everything in the oven for about 5 minutes.
- Serve immediately with a topping of sour cream and pimentos.

Amount per serving: 4

Timing Information:

Preparation	15 mins
Total Time	20 mins

Nutritional Information:

Calories	604.0
Fat	32.6g
Cholesterol	72.8mg
Sodium	977.8mg
Carbohydrates	51.5g
Protein	28.1g

* Percent Daily Values are based on a 2,000 calorie diet.

ZESTY POPCORN NACHOS

Ingredients

- 8 C. popcorn, warm
- 2 tbsp butter
- 1/2 tsp dried chives
- 1/2 tsp lime zest, finely grated
- 1/2 tsp ground cumin
- 1/2 tsp chili powder
- 1/4 tsp salt
- 1/4 tsp pepper
- 1/3 C. Monterey jack cheese, finely grated

Directions

- Set your oven to 300 degrees F before doing anything else.
- In a large rimmed baking sheet, place the popcorn evenly.
- In a microwave safe bowl, mix together the butter, lime zest, chives, chili powder and cumin and microwave on medium for about 40 seconds.
- Stir everything well and pour the mix over the popcorn with some salt and black pepper, then toss to coat well.
- Top everything with the cheese and cook the dish in the oven for about 5 minutes.

Amount per serving: 1

Timing Information:

Preparation	5 mins
Total Time	11 mins

Nutritional Information:

Calories	44.1
Fat	4.3g
Cholesterol	11.8mg
Sodium	126.2mg
Carbohydrates	0.2g
Protein	1.2g

* Percent Daily Values are based on a 2,000 calorie diet.

HOLIDAY NACHO CASSEROLE

Ingredients

- 4 C. nacho chips
- 1 C. salsa
- 1/2 C. sliced olive
- 1/2 C. green pepper, chopped
- 1/2 C. red pepper, chopped
- 1/2 C. green onion, chopped
- 1/4 C. chopped ham
- 1/2 C. cheddar cheese, grated
- 1/2 C. mozzarella cheese

Directions

- Set your oven to 350 degrees F before doing anything else.
- In a large baking sheet, place the nachos, followed by the olives, bell peppers, onions, ham and cheese.
- Cook everything in the oven till the cheese melts.

Amount per serving: 4

Timing Information:

Preparation	20 mins
Total Time	30 mins

Nutritional Information:

Calories	161.1
Fat	10.3g
Cholesterol	30.4mg
Sodium	846.0mg
Carbohydrates	8.5g
Protein	10.2g

* Percent Daily Values are based on a 2,000 calorie diet.

AMERICAN STYLE NACHOS

Ingredients

Crispas

- 2 tortillas, cut each into 8 wedges
- 1 tbsp cinnamon
- 1/2 C. sugar
- 2 C. vegetable oil
- Apple Pie Mix
- 2 baking apples, diced into 1/2 inch pieces

- 4 tsp fresh lemon juice
- 2 tbsp brown sugar
- 1 oz. Amaretto

Toppings

- 1 C. heavy whipping cream
- 1/4 C. sugar
- 1 tsp vanilla
- 1/4 C. pecans, chopped

Directions

- In a shallow dish, mix together the sugar and cinnamon.
- In a large skillet, heat the oil and fry the tortilla wedges in batches for about 1 minute, flipping once half way throughout the cooking time.
- With a slotted spoon, transfer the wedges into the sugar mixture and coat them evenly.

- Now, transfer the wedges onto a paper towel lined plate to drain and let them cool.
- In a bowl, mix together the apple and lemon juice.
- In a nonstick skillet, place the apples and amaretto on medium heat and cook them till the apples become tender.
- Stir in the brown sugar completely and remove everything from the heat.
- In a chilled bowl, add the whipping cream and beat till stiff peaks form.
- On serving plates, place 1 tortilla wedge and top each one with 1 tsp of the apple mixture, followed by 1 dollop of the whipped cream.
- Serve with a topping of the pecans.

Amount per serving: 2

Timing Information:

Preparation	15 mins
Total Time	45 mins

Nutritional Information:

Calories	3081.6
Fat	277.6g
Cholesterol	163.0mg
Sodium	498.3mg
Carbohydrates	152.4g
Protein	10.0g

* Percent Daily Values are based on a 2,000 calorie diet.

NACHOS ICELANDIC STYLE

Ingredients

- ¾ lb nacho chips
- ¼ lb grained cheese
- 1 C. salsa, sauce (hot)
- 1 avocado, peeled, pitted and mashed

Directions

- Set your oven to 350 degrees F before doing anything else.
- In a baking dish, place about 2/3 of the nachos.
- Top each nacho with a dash of salsa, followed by half of the cheese and mashed avocado.
- Place the remaining nachos on top followed by the remaining cheese.
- Cook everything in the oven till cheese melts completely.

Amount per serving: 4

Timing Information:

Preparation	5 mins
Total Time	20 mins

Nutritional Information:

Calories	758.0
Fat	48.3g
Cholesterol	29.0mg
Sodium	1706.2mg
Carbohydrates	68.7g
Protein	15.8g

* Percent Daily Values are based on a 2,000 calorie diet.

MUSHROOM PICANTE NACHOS

Ingredients

- 40 tortilla chips
- 1/3 C. sharp cheddar cheese, chopped finely
- 1/3 C. mozzarella cheese, chopped finely
- 1/2 orange bell pepper, julienned
- 1/2 green pepper, julienned
- 1 C. mushroom, diced
- 1/3 C. Pace Picante Sauce
- 1/2 tsp garlic powder

Directions

- In a microwave safe platter, place the tortillas, followed by the cheese and the remaining ingredients and microwave everything on high for about 1-2 minutes.
- Serve warm.

Amount per serving: 4

Timing Information:

Preparation	5 mins
Total Time	5 mins

Nutritional Information:

Calories	1355.8
Fat	66.1g
Cholesterol	17.2mg
Sodium	1343.0mg
Carbohydrates	174.5g
Protein	25.8g

* Percent Daily Values are based on a 2,000 calorie diet.

GRADUATION NACHOS

Ingredients

- 1 tbsp olive oil or 1 tbsp vegetable oil
- 1 C. green bell pepper, chopped
- 1 C. zucchini, chopped
- 1 C. pinto beans in chili sauce (15-oz.)
- 1 C. thick & chunky salsa
- 4 oz. tortilla chips
- 1 1/2 C. Monterey jack cheese, shredded
- ripe olives, sliced, if desired

Directions

- In a large skillet, heat the oil on high heat and sauté the zucchini and bell pepper for about 2 minutes.
- Stir in half of the salsa and beans and cook till heated through.
- Transfer the beans mixture in a large bowl.
- With a paper towel, wipe the skillet.
- In the same skillet, place the tortilla chips in a single layer and top them with the beans mixture and cheese.
- Cook, covered on medium-high heat for about 5 minutes.
- Top with the olives and remove everything from the heat.
- Serve with a topping of the remaining salsa.

Amount per serving: 4

Timing Information:

Preparation	10 mins
Total Time	17 mins

Nutritional Information:

Calories	345.2
Fat	22.5g
Cholesterol	37.7mg
Sodium	728.7mg
Carbohydrates	24.0g
Protein	14.0g

* Percent Daily Values are based on a 2,000 calorie diet.

SUPER-FAST NACHO DIP

Ingredients

- 1 (10 3/4 oz.) cans condensed cheddar cheese soup
- 1/2 C. salsa
- tortilla chips

Directions

- In a large microwave safe bowl, mix together the salsa and soup and microwave everything on high for about 2 minutes, stirring once half way through the cooking time.
- Serve the dish as a dipping sauce alongside the tortilla chips.

Amount per serving: 1

Timing Information:

Preparation	1 min
Total Time	3 mins

Nutritional Information:

Calories	201.9
Fat	12.5g
Cholesterol	35.0mg
Sodium	1444.9mg
Carbohydrates	16.5g
Protein	7.4g

* Percent Daily Values are based on a 2,000 calorie diet.

TASTIER KALE CHIPS

Ingredients

- 1 bunch kale, trimmed and hard stalks removed
- 1 C. cashews, soak for a few hours
- 1/4 C. lemon juice
- 1/3 C. nutritional yeast
- 1 tsp salt
- 1 tsp cumin
- 1 tsp chili powder
- 1 tsp garlic powder

Directions

- In a blender, add all the ingredients except the kale and pulse till smooth. (Add a little bit of water if required.)
- Transfer the mixture into a large bowl with the kale and mix till well combined.
- Transfer the Kale leaves onto a parchment paper lined dehydrator tray on low.
- Dehydrate for about 10 hours.

Amount per serving: 4

Timing Information:

Preparation	5 mins
Total Time	35 mins

Nutritional Information:

Calories	283.4
Fat	17.7g
Cholesterol	0.0mg
Sodium	842.9mg
Carbohydrates	25.0g
Protein	13.7g

* Percent Daily Values are based on a 2,000 calorie diet.

Nachos Mediterranean Style

Ingredients

- 2 tbsp finely chopped kalamata olives
- 2 tbsp finely chopped sun-dried tomatoes packed in oil (from 7 oz. jar)
- 2 tsp oil from jar sun-dried tomatoes
- 1 small plum tomato, finely chopped and drained
- 1 medium green onion, thinly sliced (1 T)
- 4 oz. restaurant-style corn tortilla chips
- 1 (4 oz.) packages feta cheese, finely crumbled

Directions

- In a bowl, mix together all the ingredients except the tortilla chips and cheese.
- In a microwave safe platter, place the tortilla chips in a single layer and top them with the cheese and microwave everything on high for about 1 minute.
- Rotate the plate and continue microwaving for about 30-60 seconds more.
- Top everything with the vegetables mixture and serve.

Amount per serving: 6

Timing Information:

Preparation	10 mins
Total Time	10 mins

Nutritional Information:

Calories	156.8
Fat	9.3g
Cholesterol	17.8mg
Sodium	342.3mg
Carbohydrates	14.6g
Protein	4.6g

* Percent Daily Values are based on a 2,000 calorie diet.

MEXICAN MACHO BAKE

Ingredients

- 1 1/2 lb. ground beef, cooked
- 1/2 can refried beans
- 16 oz. sour cream
- 8 oz. shredded cheddar cheese
- 1 bag tortilla chips, crushed

Directions

- Set your oven to 350 degrees F before doing anything else.
- In a bowl, mix together the beans and beef.
- Transfer the beef mixture into a casserole dish, followed by the sour cream, cheese.
- With foil, cover the casserole dish and cook everything in the oven for about 15-20 minutes.
- Uncover and top everything with the crushed tortilla chips.
- Cook everything in the oven for about 5 minutes.

Amount per serving: 6

Timing Information:

Preparation	15 mins
Total Time	35 mins

Nutritional Information:

Calories	740.0
Fat	54.5g
Cholesterol	151.8mg
Sodium	501.3mg
Carbohydrates	27.0g
Protein	35.7g

* Percent Daily Values are based on a 2,000 calorie diet.

CREAMY CINNAMON CARAMEL AND MANGO NACHOS

Ingredients

Cinnamon Cream

- 1 C. whipping cream
- 2 -3 tbsp sugar
- 1/8 tsp cinnamon

Nachos

- 6 fajita-size flour tortillas, cut each into 6 wedges
- oil (for frying)
- 1/4 C. sugar
- 1 tsp cinnamon
- 1/2 C. caramel sauce
- 1 1/2 C. diced mangoes

Directions

- For the cinnamon cream, in a bowl, add all the ingredients and beat till stiff peaks form.
- Transfer the cream into a serving bowl and refrigerate.
- For the nachos, in a skillet, heat the oil and fry the wedges in batches till golden brown.
- With a slotted spoon, transfer everything onto a paper towel lined plate to drain.

- In a bowl, mix together the cinnamon and sugar.
- Add fried wedges and toss to coat well and arrange into a serving platter.
- In a microwave safe bowl, place the caramel sauce and microwave on high for about 20-30 seconds.
- Pour the sauce over the wedges and top with the chopped mango.
- Serve with a topping of cinnamon cream.

Amount per serving: 4

Timing Information:

Preparation	15 mins
Total Time	35 mins

Nutritional Information:

Calories	752.9
Fat	30.3g
Cholesterol	81.9mg
Sodium	837.7mg
Carbohydrates	112.9g
Protein	10.8g

* Percent Daily Values are based on a 2,000 calorie diet.

EAST LA STYLE NACHOS

Ingredients

- 2 boneless skinless chicken breasts, cut into small strips.
- 1/2 C. lime juice
- 1 tsp pepper
- 1 tsp chili powder
- 2 tbsp olive oil
- 1 C. frozen corn kernels
- 1/3 C. red onion, chopped
- 1 tbsp lime juice
- 1 tsp cumin
- tortilla chips

Directions

- In a bowl, mix together the chicken, olive oil, 1/4 C. of the lime juice, chili powder and black pepper and refrigerate to marinate for about 30 minutes.
- Meanwhile, cook the corn till desired doneness.
- In a bowl, add the onion, corn and the remaining lime juice and toss to coat.

- Heat a large nonstick frying pan and cook the chicken till the desired doneness.
- Transfer the chicken into the bowl, with the corn mixture and mix well.
- Top the tortilla chips with the chicken mixture and serve.

Amount per serving: 4

Timing Information:

Preparation	15 mins
Total Time	1 hr

Nutritional Information:

Calories	222.6
Fat	9.1g
Cholesterol	37.7mg
Sodium	85.0mg
Carbohydrates	23.1g
Protein	15.6g

* Percent Daily Values are based on a 2,000 calorie diet.

Tex-Mex Nachos

Ingredients

- 1 whole wheat pita bread, cut each half into 8 triangles
- 1/4 avocado
- 1 tomatoes
- 30 g low-fat cheese
- ground black pepper
- 1/4 C. coriander

Directions

- Set your oven to 355 degrees F before doing anything else.
- In 2 large baking sheets, place the pita triangles in a single layer and cook everything in the oven for about 5 minutes.
- In a bowl, mix together the tomato, avocado, 1 tbsp of the cheese, salt and black pepper.
- In 2 small baking dishes, divide the tomato mixture evenly.
- Divide the pita triangles between both dishes and gently, push in the tomato mixture, then sprinkle with the remaining cheese.
- Cook everything in the oven for about 5 minutes.
- Serve with a garnishing of the cilantro.

Amount per serving: 2

Timing Information:

Preparation	10 mins
Total Time	20 mins

Nutritional Information:

Calories	162.8
Fat	5.7g
Cholesterol	3.1mg
Sodium	267.7mg
Carbohydrates	22.5g
Protein	7.8g

* Percent Daily Values are based on a 2,000 calorie diet.

SUPER-QUICK NACHO DIP

Ingredients

- 1 bag tortilla chips
- 1 can Frito-Lay bean dip
- shredded cheddar cheese
- jalapeno, sliced

Directions

- Set the broiler of your oven and line a baking sheet with foil.
- Place the tortilla chips onto the prepared cookie sheet in a single layer and top each one with the bean dip, followed by the cheese and jalapeño slices.
- Cook under broiler till the cheese is melted.

Amount per serving: 1

Timing Information:

Preparation	20 mins
Total Time	25 mins

Nutritional Information:

Calories	1039.4
Fat	49.7g
Cholesterol	0.0mg
Sodium	896.7mg
Carbohydrates	139.1g
Protein	16.5g

* Percent Daily Values are based on a 2,000 calorie diet.

Extra Lean Cheese Whiz Nachos

Ingredients

- 1 lb. extra lean ground beef
- 7 C. tortilla chips
- 1/2 lb. Velveeta cheese, pasteurized prepared cheese product cut into 1/2-inch cubes
- 1 C. shredded lettuce
- 1/2 C. chopped tomato
- 1/4 C. sliced black olives
- 1/3 C. sour cream

Directions

- Heat a large skillet and cook the beef till cooked completely done, and drain the fat completely.
- In a large microwave safe platter, place the tortilla chips and top everything with the Velveeta cheese and microwave on high for about 2 minutes.
- In a bowl, mix together the beef and remaining ingredients.
- Place the beef mixture over the chips and serve.

Amount per serving: 4

Timing Information:

Preparation	5 mins
Total Time	5 mins

Nutritional Information:

Calories	381.0
Fat	22.9g
Cholesterol	123.5mg
Sodium	1001.3mg
Carbohydrates	7.9g
Protein	34.4g

* Percent Daily Values are based on a 2,000 calorie diet.

Southwest Neufchatel Nacho Soup

Ingredients

Soup

- 2 lb. lean ground beef
- salt (or to taste)
- 1/2 tsp pepper
- 4 C. beef broth
- 10 oz. diced tomatoes and green chilies
- 6 oz. neufchatel cheese, cut into cubes
- 6 oz. Velveeta cheese, cut into cubes
- Garnish
- shredded cheese
- sour cream
- hot sauce

Directions

- Heat a large soup pan and cook the beef until it is browned completely. Drain the fat from the skillet and stir in the salt and black pepper. Add the tomatoes and broth and bring everything to a boil. Simmer, covered for about 15 minutes. Stir in the Velveeta cheese and cream cheese and cook on medium-low heat till the cheese melts. Serve with a topping of sour cream, shredded cheese and hot sauce.

Amount per serving: 8

Timing Information:

Preparation	5 mins
Total Time	30 mins

Nutritional Information:

Calories	330.5
Fat	21.3g
Cholesterol	107.0mg
Sodium	1484.3mg
Carbohydrates	3.9g
Protein	29.4g

* Percent Daily Values are based on a 2,000 calorie diet.

PICNIC NACHOS

Ingredients

- white corn tortilla chips
- 1 lb. zesty hot sausage
- 1 lb. ground beef
- 2 (4 oz.) cans mild green chilies
- 1 (1 1/4 oz.) packets taco seasoning
- 2 C. salsa
- 1 bunch green onion, chopped
- 4 C. shredded Mexican blend cheese
- 8 oz. sour cream
- aluminum foil
- cooking spray

Directions

- Cut a sheet of foil into 4 sheets to make packets that will cover the tortilla chips with toppings.
- Grease each foil sheet with the cooking spray.
- Divide the nacho chips in the middle of each foil sheet.
- Place your desired toppings over the nacho chips.

- Fold the foil around the filling to make packets.
- Place the packets onto a grill over a low burning campfire.
- Cook over the campfire for about 10-15 minutes.
- Serve with a topping of sour cream.

Amount per serving: 4

Timing Information:

Preparation	15 mins
Total Time	30 mins

Nutritional Information:

Calories	1612.3
Fat	129.7g
Cholesterol	405.8mg
Sodium	4498.4mg
Carbohydrates	21.8g
Protein	88.6g

* Percent Daily Values are based on a 2,000 calorie diet.

Slow Cooker Nachos

Ingredients

- 1 lb. lean ground beef
- 2 -3 cloves garlic, minced
- 2 (16 oz.) packages Velveeta Mexican cheese, cut into cubes
- 2 (10 oz.) cans Rotel Tomatoes, drained
- 1/2 C. chopped green onion
- tortilla chips

Directions

- Heat a large skillet and cook the beef and garlic until it is browned completely.
- Drain the fat from the skillet.
- Transfer the beef mixture in a large slow cooker with the tomatoes and cheese and stir to combine.
- Set the slow cooker on Low and cook, covered for about 3-4 hours, stirring once after 2 hours.
- Uncover and stir in the onions.
- Serve the beef mixture with the tortilla chips.

Amount per serving: 15

Timing Information:

Preparation	20 mins
Total Time	4 hrs 20 mins

Nutritional Information:

Calories	241.5
Fat	16.2g
Cholesterol	67.4mg
Sodium	1067.5mg
Carbohydrates	7.6g
Protein	16.1g

* Percent Daily Values are based on a 2,000 calorie diet.

ENCHILADA AND NACHOS

Ingredients

- 1 C. enchilada sauce
- 1 lb. tortilla chips
- 2 (16 oz.) cans refried beans, heated
- 1 -2 C. shredded cheddar cheese
- 1 C. sour cream

Directions

- Divide the tortilla chips in serving plates.
- Serve with the remaining ingredients as nachos.

Amount per serving: 6

Timing Information:

Preparation	5 mins
Total Time	10 mins

Nutritional Information:

Calories	672.6
Fat	34.0g
Cholesterol	48.7mg
Sodium	973.7mg
Carbohydrates	75.2g
Protein	20.1g

* Percent Daily Values are based on a 2,000 calorie diet.

SWEET PAPRIKA NACHOS

Ingredients

- 1/2 lb. ground beef
- 1 tsp chili powder (Mexican blend)
- 1/2 tsp salt
- 1/2 tsp dried onion flakes
- 1/8 tsp sweet paprika
- 2 tbsp water
- 8 restaurant-style corn tortilla chips
- 1/2 C. refried beans
- 1 1/2 C. shredded cheddar cheese
- 1/2 C. shredded monterey jack cheese
- 1/4 C. diced onion
- 1 large jalapeno pepper

Directions

- Set your oven to 375 degrees F before doing anything else.
- Heat a large skillet and cook the beef until it is browned completely.
- Drain the fat from the skillet.

- Add the dried onion, paprika, chili powder, salt and water and reduce the heat to low.
- Simmer for about 10 minutes.
- In a pan, add the beans and cook till heated through.
- In a small bowl, mix together the both cheeses.
- In a large pie plate, place the tortilla chips.
- Place about 1 tbsp of the beans over each chip, followed by about 2 tbsp of the beef mixture, cheese mixture, onion and 1 slice of jalapeño pepper.
- Cook everything in the oven for about 8-10 minutes.

Amount per serving: 4

Timing Information:

Preparation	10 mins
Total Time	30 mins

Nutritional Information:

Calories	634.3
Fat	39.4g
Cholesterol	95.6mg
Sodium	1031.3mg
Carbohydrates	40.9g
Protein	30.4g

* Percent Daily Values are based on a 2,000 calorie diet.

NACHOS JAMAICAN STYLE

Ingredients

- jamaican jerk spice
- 1 red bell pepper, seeded and chopped finely
- 1 yellow bell pepper, seeded and chopped finely
- 2 boneless skinless chicken breasts, boiled and chopped
- 1 lemon
- 1 (12 1/2 oz.) bags taco flavor Doritos
- 2 C. four-cheese Mexican blend cheese

Directions

- Set your oven to 400 degrees F before doing anything else.
- Coat the chicken with about 3 tbsp of the jerk spice.
- In a bowl, mix together the bell peppers and lemon juice.
- In the bottom of a large baking dish, place 1 bag of the Doritos, followed by the chicken and cheese.
- Cook everything in the oven till the cheese is melted.
- Just before serving, add the bell peppers and mix.

Amount per serving: 4

Timing Information:

Preparation	30 mins
Total Time	40 mins

Nutritional Information:

Calories	336.7
Fat	20.7g
Cholesterol	103.5mg
Sodium	787.1mg
Carbohydrates	10.6g
Protein	28.8g

* Percent Daily Values are based on a 2,000 calorie diet.

Zucchini Nachos

Ingredients

- 4 -5 C. zucchini, sliced
- 1 small onion, diced
- 2 tbsp chili peppers (chopped)
- 1 tbsp butter
- 1 (10 oz.) can cream of celery soup
- 8 oz. monterey jack cheese, shredded
- 2 C. nacho cheese flavor Doritos, crushed
- salt and pepper

Directions

- Set your oven to 350 degrees F before doing anything else and grease a large casserole dish.
- In the bottom of the prepared casserole dish, place the zucchini slices.
- In a large skillet, melt the butter and sauté the onion till tender.
- Transfer the onion over zucchini evenly, followed by 2 tbsp of the chilies.

- In a bowl, mix together the cheese and celery soup and pour over the zucchini mixture.
- Cover the casserole dish with the foil and cook everything in the oven for about 45 minutes.
- Uncover and top the casserole with the Doritos.
- Cook everything in the oven for about 5 minutes more.

Amount per serving: 6

Timing Information:

| Preparation | 15 mins |
| Total Time | 1 hr 15 mins |

Nutritional Information:

Calories	218.9
Fat	16.3g
Cholesterol	45.9mg
Sodium	594.9mg
Carbohydrates	7.6g
Protein	11.5g

* Percent Daily Values are based on a 2,000 calorie diet.

GOURMET NACHOS

Ingredients

- 6 -7 oz. tortilla chips
- 2 C. cheddar cheese, grated
- 3 oz. cured chorizo sausage, chopped
- 1 C. frozen corn, thawed
- 1/2 C. pickled jalapeno pepper

Directions

- Set your oven to 450 degrees F before doing anything else and line a baking sheet with foil.
- In the bottom of the prepared baking sheet, place the tortilla chips, followed by the cheese, chorizo and corn.
- Cook everything in the oven for about 3-5 minutes.
- Serve with a topping of jalapeño peppers.

Amount per serving: 6

Timing Information:

Preparation	10 mins
Total Time	15 mins

Nutritional Information:

Calories	370.8
Fat	24.3g
Cholesterol	52.0mg
Sodium	708.9mg
Carbohydrates	24.0g
Protein	15.7g

* Percent Daily Values are based on a 2,000 calorie diet.

Nachos Italian Style

Ingredients

- 1 baguette, sliced into 1/2-inch rounds
- olive oil
- 3 C. Fontina cheese, shredded, 1/2 lb.
- 2 C. tomatoes, seeded, diced
- 1/2 C. pepperoncini pepper, sliced

Directions

- Set your oven to 400 degrees F before doing anything else.
- In a baking sheet, place the baguette rounds and cook everything in the oven for about 5-6 minutes.
- Now, set the oven to broiler.
- Drizzle the baguette rounds with oil evenly and sprinkle them with salt.
- Cook everything under the broiler for about 2-3 minutes.
- Sprinkle the nachos with the Fontina cheese and continue cooking them under the broiler for about 2-3 minutes.
- Top everything with the pepperoncini and tomatoes and serve immediately.

Amount per serving: 6

Timing Information:

Preparation	15 mins
Total Time	15 mins

Nutritional Information:

Calories	430.3
Fat	19.2g
Cholesterol	62.6mg
Sodium	1028.3mg
Carbohydrates	43.0g
Protein	21.1g

* Percent Daily Values are based on a 2,000 calorie diet.

NACHOS IRISH STYLE

Ingredients

- vegetable oil, as required
- 5 potatoes, sliced thick with skin on
- 5 slices bacon, cooked and crumbled
- 6 slices cheddar cheese, chopped
- 4 pickled jalapenos, sliced
- 1/4 sweet onion, chopped
- 1 -2 tbsp seasoning salt

Directions

- Set the broiler of your oven before doing anything else.
- In a skillet, heat the oil and fry the potatoes till golden brown.
- Transfer the potatoes onto a paper towel lined plate to drain.
- Sprinkle everything with the seasoning salt.
- In an oven proof skillet, place the potatoes, followed by the cheddar cheese, bacon, onion and jalapeño peppers and cook everything under the broiler for about 10-15 minutes.
- Add the sour cream, scallions, tomatoes, and more jalapenos for extra taste.

Amount per serving: 4

Timing Information:

Preparation	20 mins
Total Time	32 mins

Nutritional Information:

Calories	426.8
Fat	18.7g
Cholesterol	50.9mg
Sodium	360.7mg
Carbohydrates	48.6g
Protein	17.2g

* Percent Daily Values are based on a 2,000 calorie diet.

HEAVY CREAM NACHO DIP

Ingredients

- 1 (435 g) can refried beans
- 1 ¼ C. heavy cream
- 1 (35 g) packets taco seasoning mix, only use 1/2 to 3/4
- 1 avocado (diced into 1cm pieces)
- 1 large tomato, ripe (diced into 1cm pieces)
- cracked pepper
- salt, to taste
- 1/2-3/4 C. cheese, grated

Directions

- In a large dish, place the refried beans.
- In a bowl, mix together the double cream and taco seasoning.
- Spread the double cream over the beans evenly, followed by the avocado and tomato.
- Sprinkle everything with salt and black pepper and top with the cheese.
- Serve alongside the corn chips.

Amount per serving: 1

Timing Information:

Preparation	20 mins
Total Time	20 mins

Nutritional Information:

Calories	1970.9
Fat	161.6g
Cholesterol	455.3mg
Sodium	2529.7mg
Carbohydrates	100.1g
Protein	45.2g

* Percent Daily Values are based on a 2,000 calorie diet.

MICROWAVE MEXICAN LASAGNA NACHOS

Ingredients

- 11 oz lasagna noodles
- 1 lb lean ground beef
- 24 oz tomato sauce
- 1/2 C. water
- 1 (1 oz) package taco seasoning mix
- 8 C. shredded Cheddar cheese
- 1/2 C. minced tortilla chips

Directions

- Boil your pasta for 10 mins in water and salt. Remove all water. Set aside.
- Fry your beef until browned, and remove excess oils. Combine in some taco seasoning, then tomato and finally water. Lightly simmer for 6 mins.
- Get your dish (must be able to fit in microwave), and layer in the following manner: lasagna noodles, beef mix, cheese. Continue until dish is full.
- Microwave for 10 mins on the highest power setting covered with plastic wrap.
- Garnish with tortilla chips.
- Enjoy.

Servings: 8 to 10 servings

Timing Information:

Preparation	Cooking	Total Time
10 mins	10 mins	25 mins

Nutritional Information:

Calories	709 kcal
Carbohydrates	35.8 g
Cholesterol	143 mg
Fat	45.4 g
Fiber	2.3 g
Protein	39.3 g
Sodium	1304 mg

* Percent Daily Values are based on a 2,000 calorie diet.

CREAM OF NACHO DIP

Ingredients

- 1 (10 3/4 oz.) cans condensed cream of mushroom soup
- 1/2 C. salsa
- tortilla chips

Directions

- In a large microwave safe bowl, mix together the salsa and soup and microwave everything on high for about 2 minutes, stirring once half way through the cooking time.
- Serve the dish as a dipping sauce alongside the tortilla chips.

Amount per serving: 1

Timing Information:

Preparation	1 min
Total Time	3 mins

Nutritional Information:

Calories	201.9
Fat	12.5g
Cholesterol	35.0mg
Sodium	1444.9mg
Carbohydrates	16.5g
Protein	7.4g

* Percent Daily Values are based on a 2,000 calorie diet.

PEPPER JACK NACHOS

Ingredients

- 1/2 lb. sliced bacon
- 36 tortilla chips
- 1 medium sweet onion (chopped)
- 6 pickled jalapeno peppers (stemmed, seeded & minced)
- 2 C. grated pepper jack cheese
- 8 oz. sour cream
- mild salsa

Directions

- Set your oven to 475 degrees F before doing anything else.
- Heat a large skillet and cook the bacon until it is browned completely.
- Transfer the bacon onto a paper towel lined plate to drain and then chop it.
- In a large rimmed baking sheet, place the tortilla chips, followed by the bacon, onions, jalapeño peppers and cheese.
- Cook everything in the oven for about 5 minutes.
- Serve alongside the sour cream and salsa.

Amount per serving: 4

Timing Information:

Preparation	15 mins
Total Time	20 mins

Nutritional Information:

Calories	1750.0
Fat	109.4g
Cholesterol	119.9mg
Sodium	2360.6mg
Carbohydrates	160.0g
Protein	40.4g

* Percent Daily Values are based on a 2,000 calorie diet.

Mozzarella Nachos

Ingredients

- 1 C. salsa
- 1 cucumber, peeled and sliced
- 1/2 C. mozzarella cheese, shredded
- 1/2 C. fat free sour cream

Directions

- In a strainer, place the salsa to drain slightly.
- In a 13x9-inch baking dish, arrange the cucumber slices in a single layer.
- Place about 1 tsp of the salsa over each cucumber slice and sprinkle each with the cheese.
- Place about 1 tsp of the sour cream over each slice and serve.

Amount per serving: 1

Timing Information:

Preparation	10 mins
Total Time	10 mins

Nutritional Information:

Calories	11.0
Fat	0.1g
Cholesterol	0.5mg
Sodium	78.6mg
Carbohydrates	2.2g
Protein	0.5g

* Percent Daily Values are based on a 2,000 calorie diet.

Thanks for Reading! Join the Club and Keep on Cooking with 6 More Cookbooks....

http://bit.ly/1TdrStv

To grab the box sets simply follow the link mentioned above, or tap one of book covers.

This will take you to a page where you can simply enter your email address and a PDF version of the box sets will be emailed to you.

Hope you are ready for some serious cooking!

http://bit.ly/1TdrStv

Come On...
Let's Be Friends :)

We adore our readers and love connecting with them socially.

Like BookSumo on Facebook and let's get social!

Facebook

And also check out the BookSumo Cooking Blog.

Food Lover Blog

Made in the USA
San Bernardino, CA
17 January 2017